Bernadett
Urbanovics

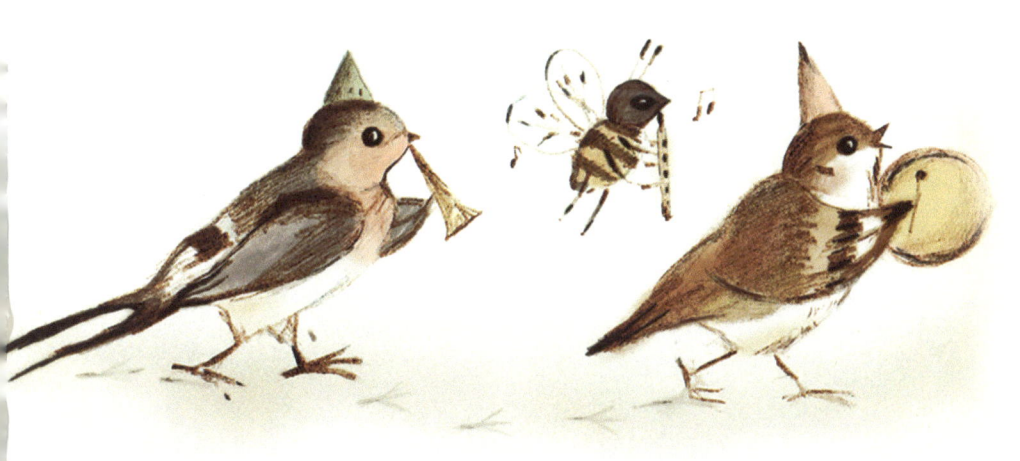

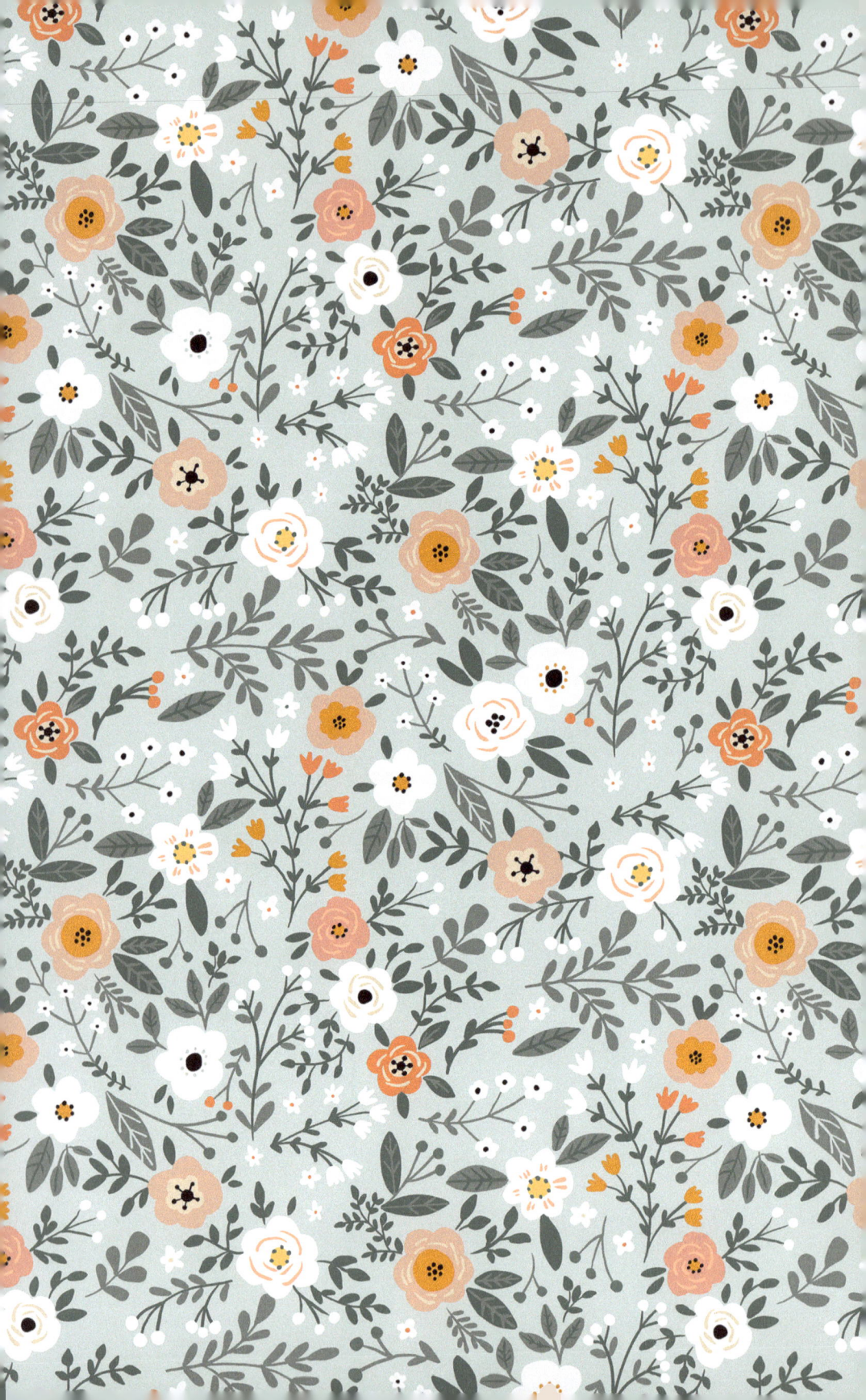

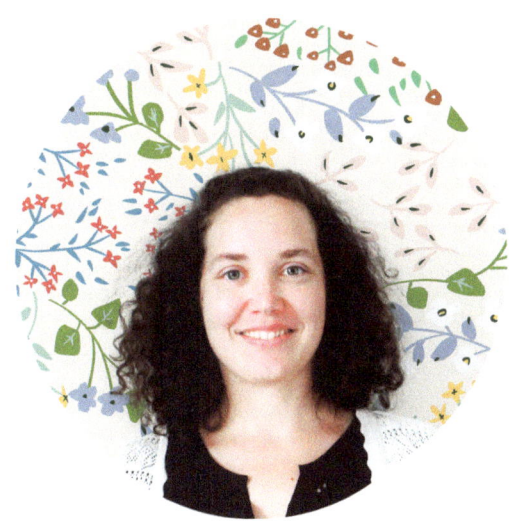

W www.bernadetturbanovics.com
◎ petitfaon_prints
P petitfaonprints

Hello! My name is Bernadett.
I am a freelance illustrator and surface pattern designer.
My educational background lies in architecture, a field that ignited my passion for design and creativity.
From 2017 I've devoted myself to creating seamless patterns and illustrations that are a reflection of my love for art, nature, and the world of childhood. My patterns often feature delicate flowers that evoke the beauty of the natural world and adorable animals that bring smiles to our faces. It's my way of contributing a touch of beauty and happiness to our surroundings.

....

You can find my works at:

Parklon
Lilipinso
Vitry Paris
FIGO Fabrics
Minted
Spoonflower
Decore Imprime
KASEME
Inch blue
Little Buck

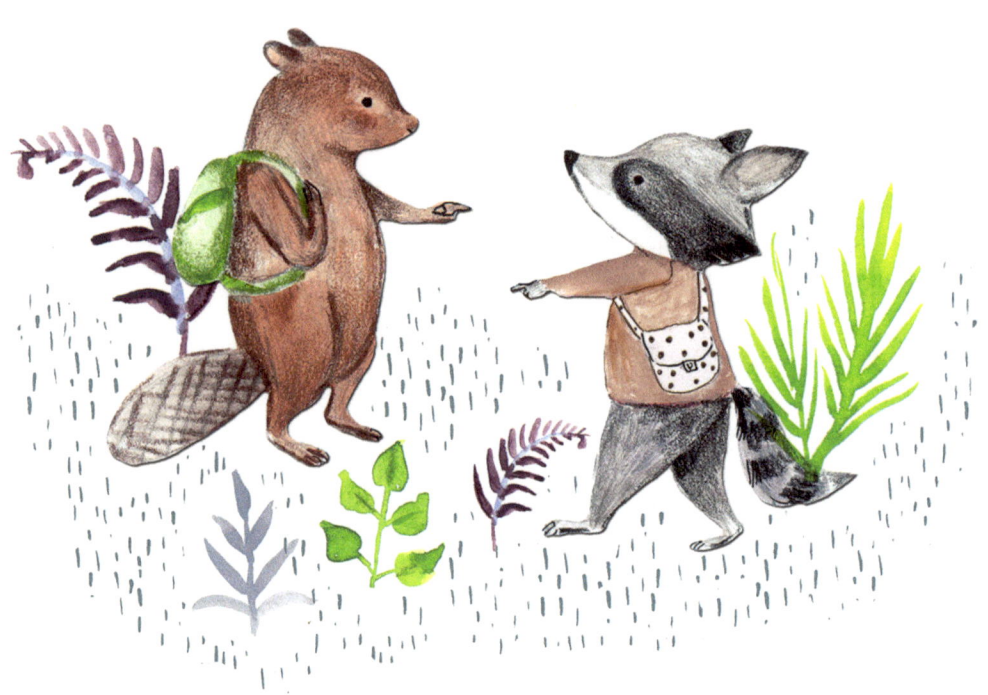

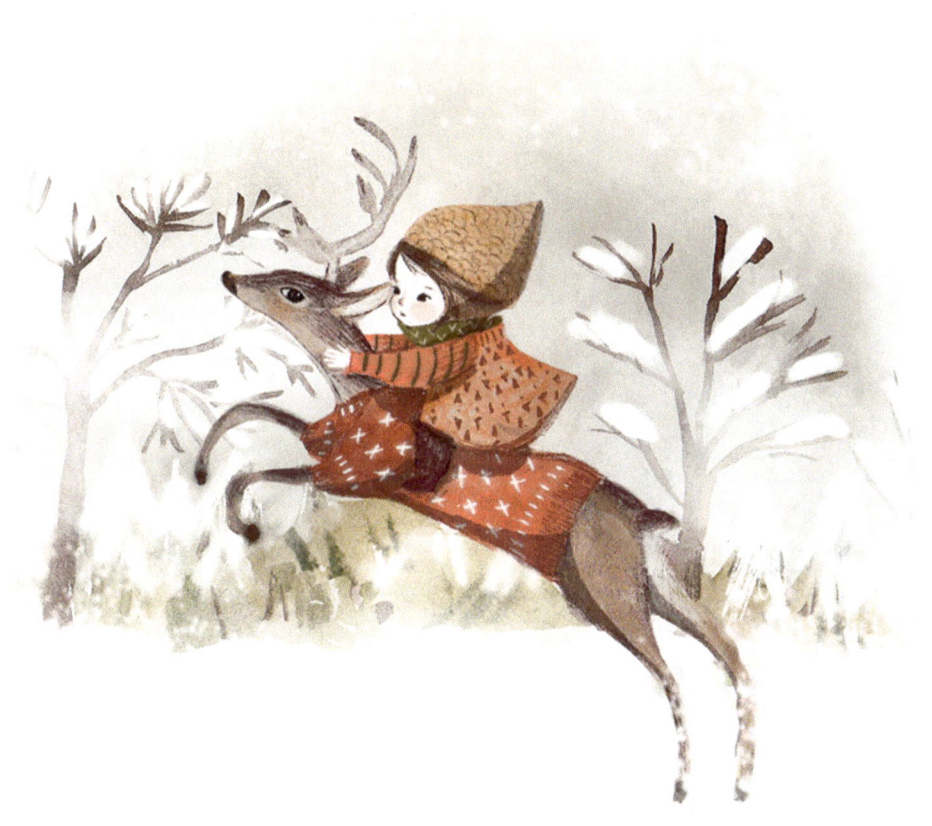

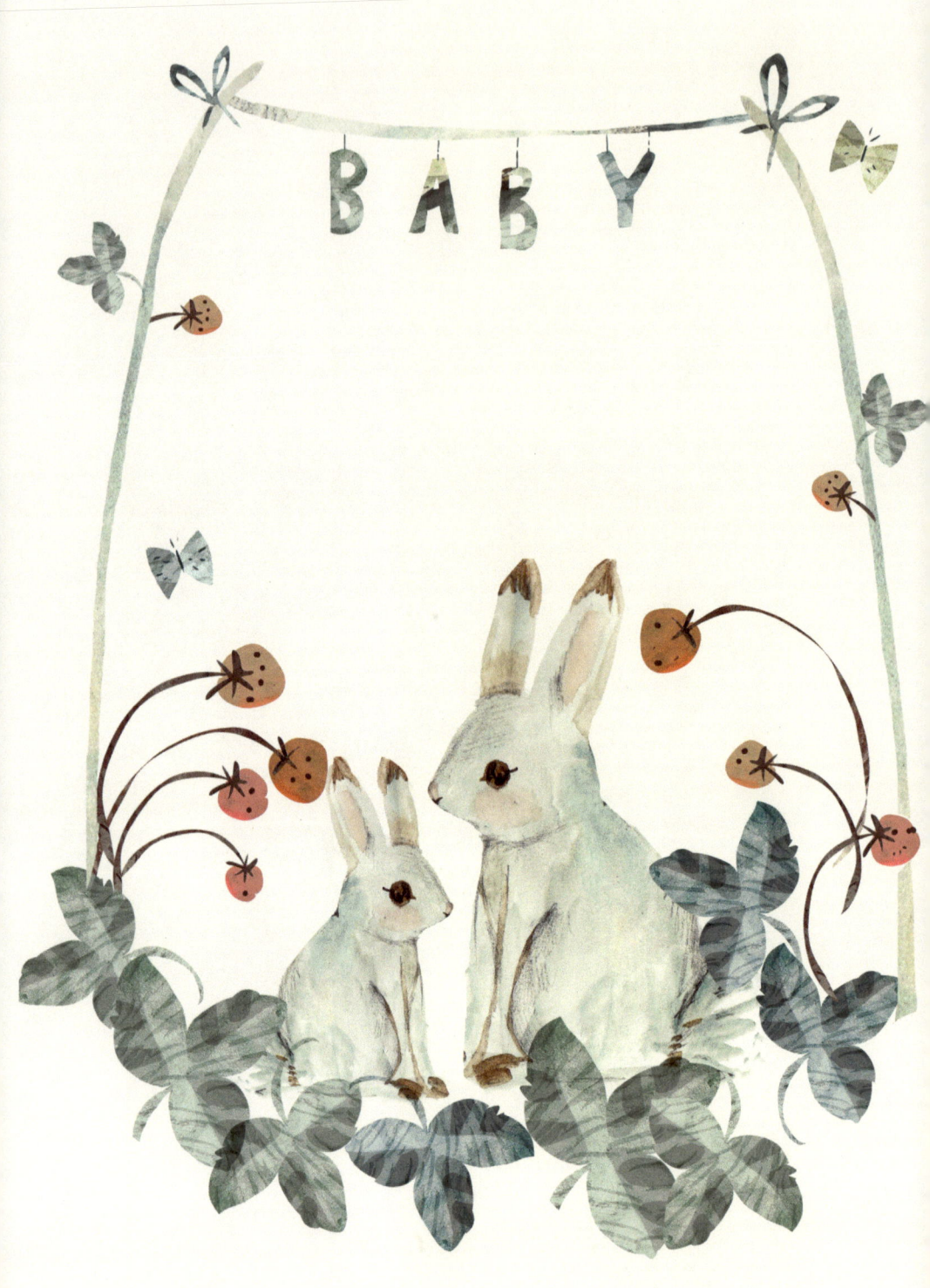

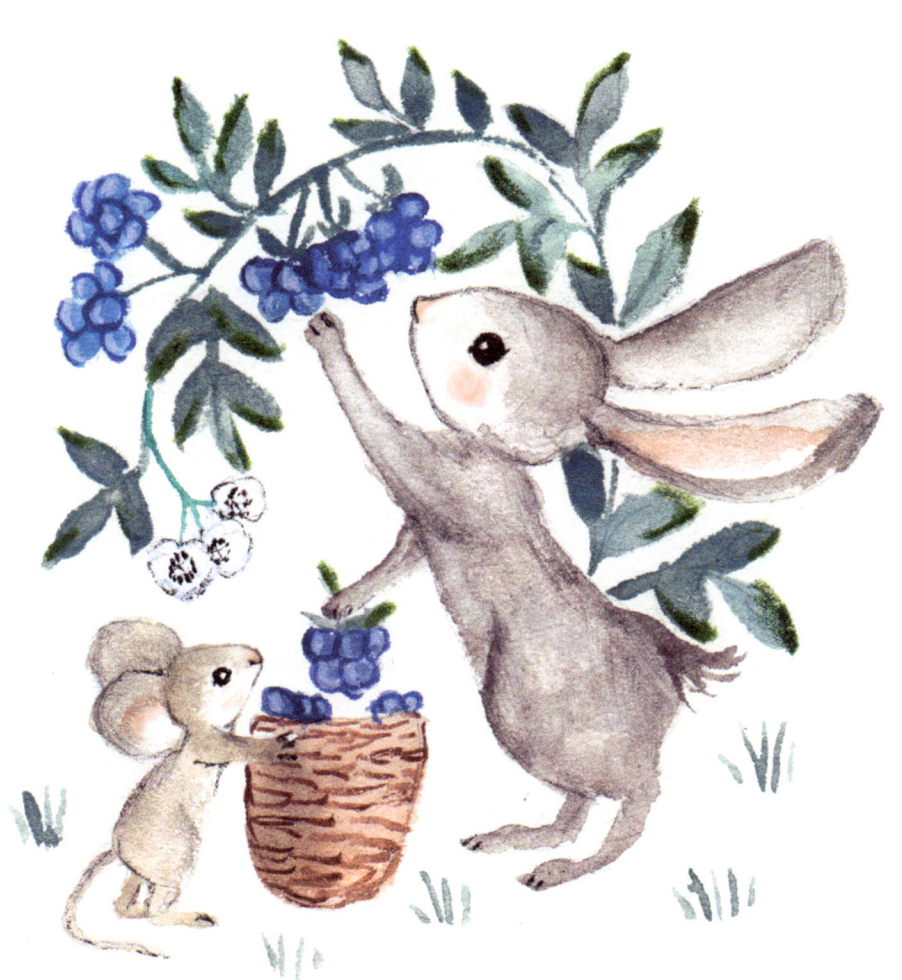

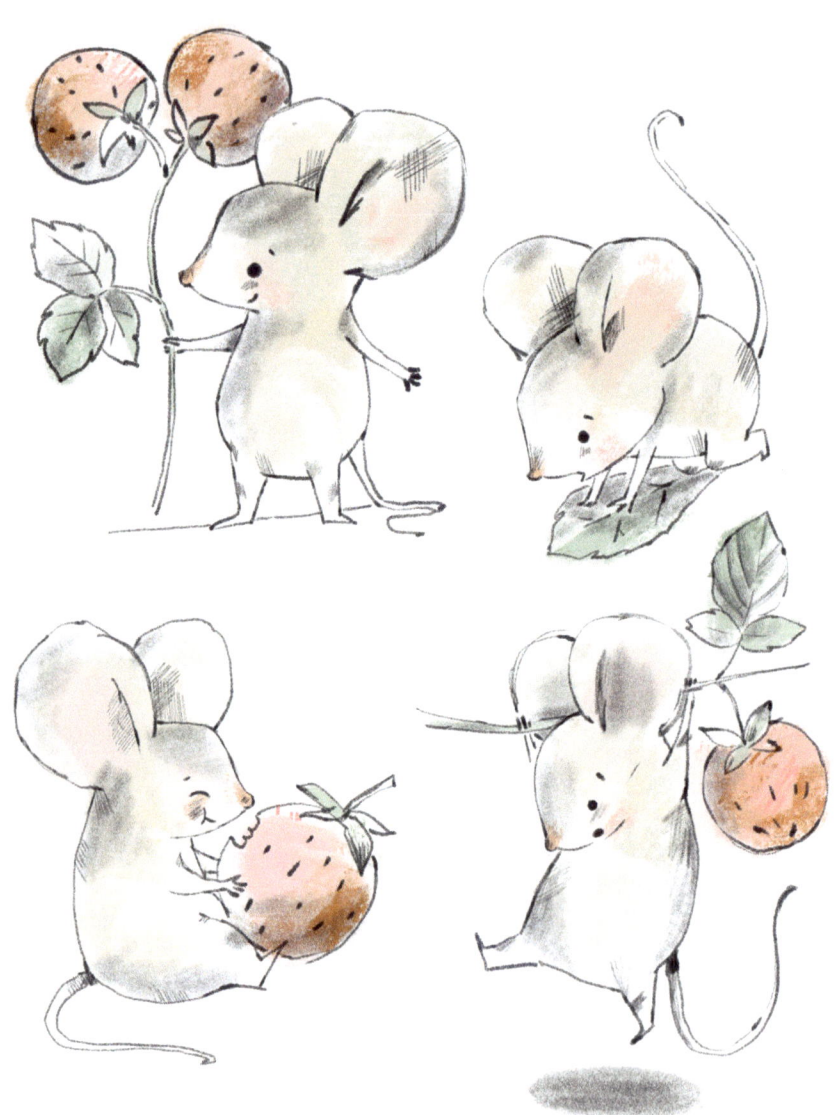

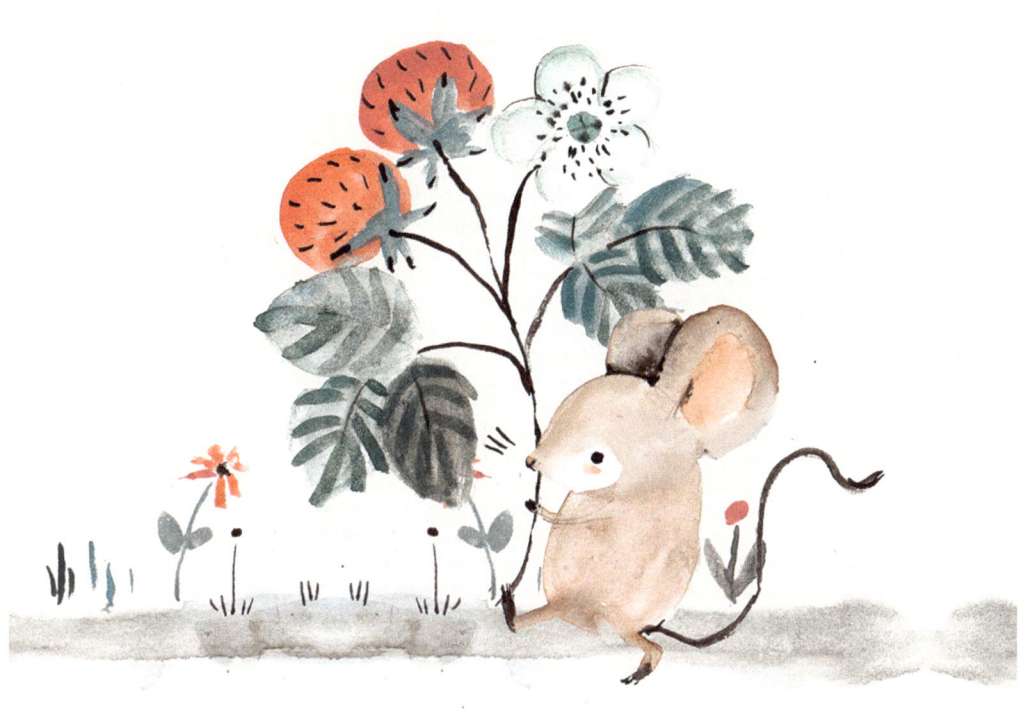

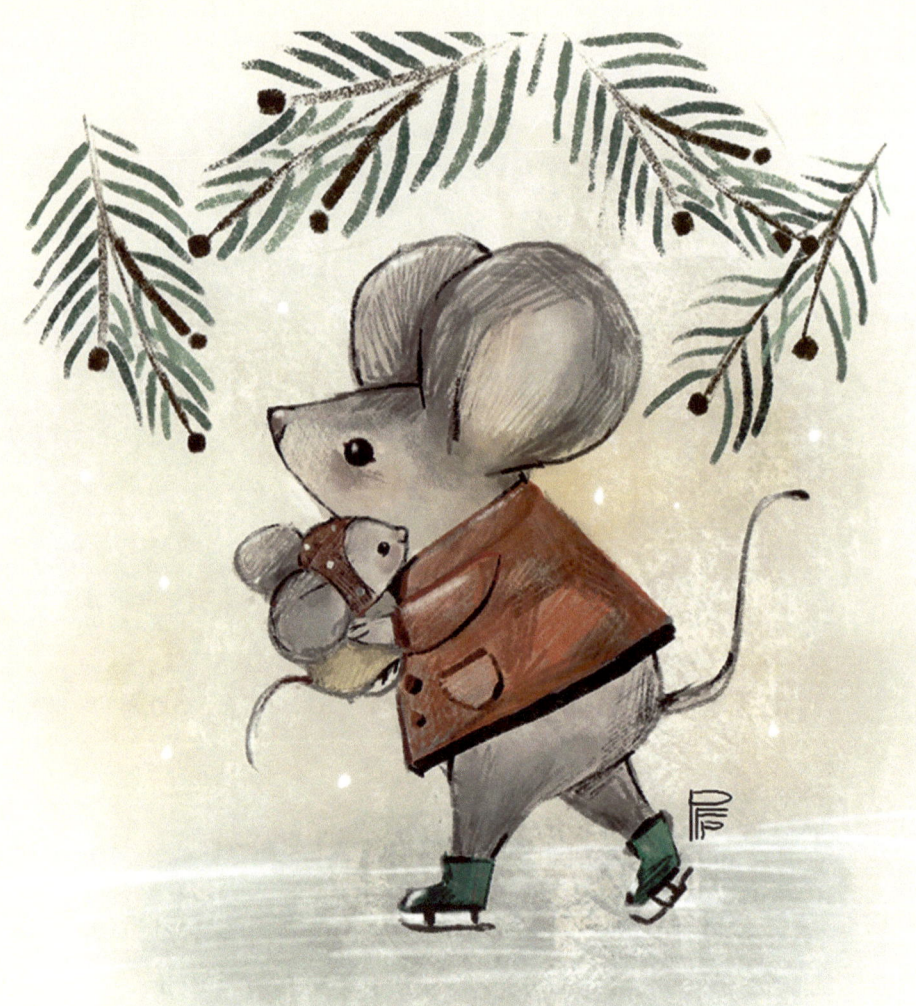

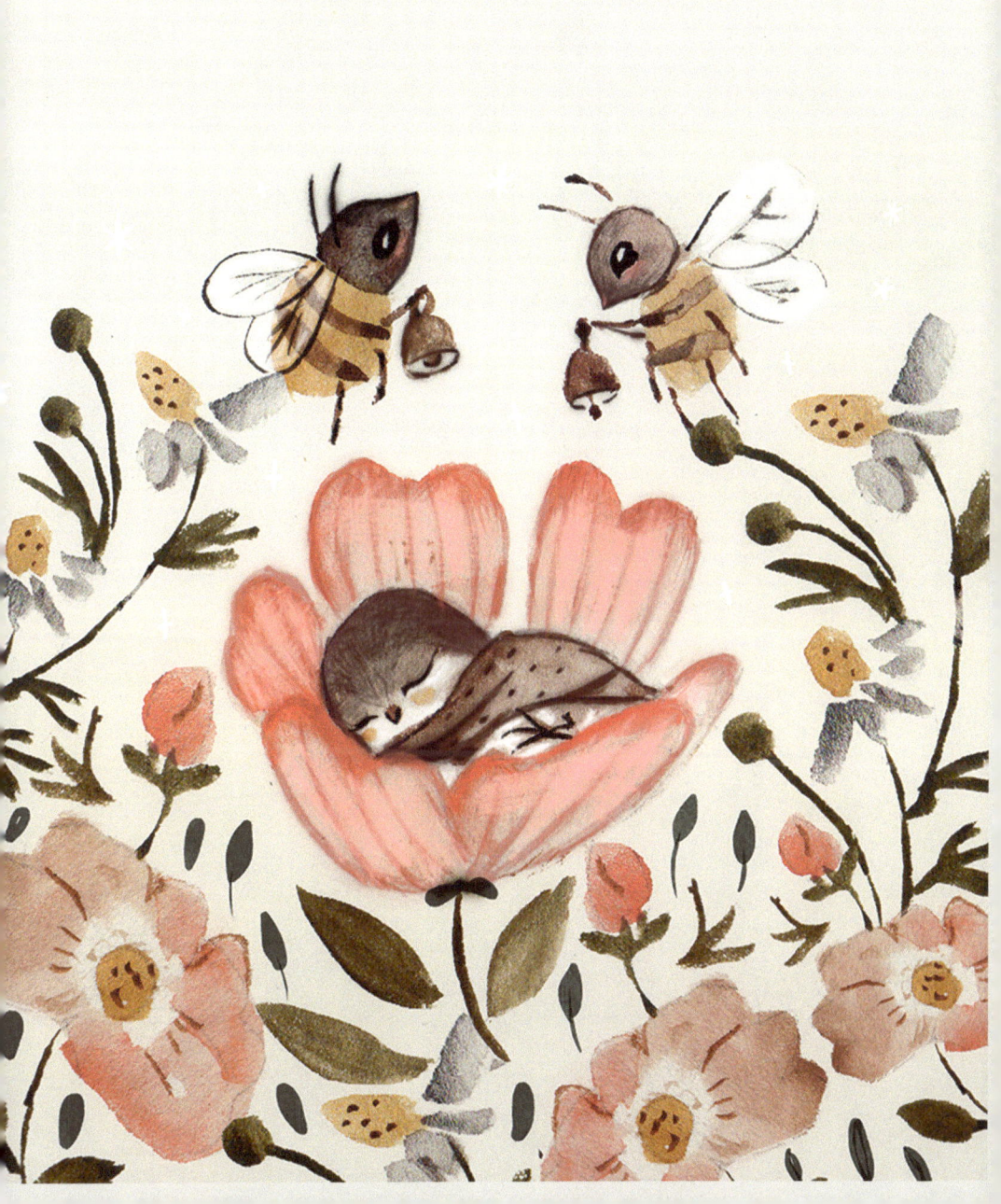

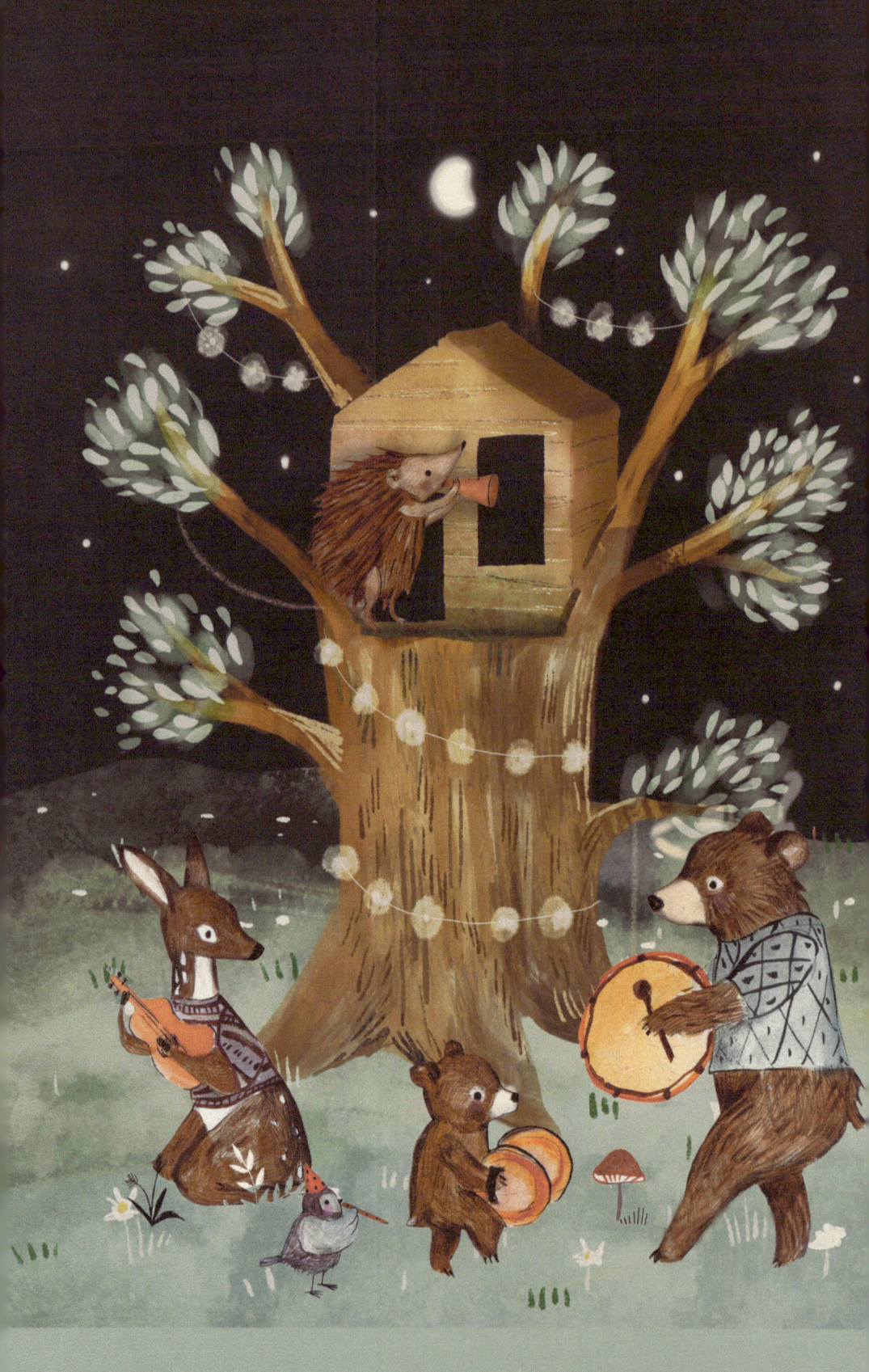

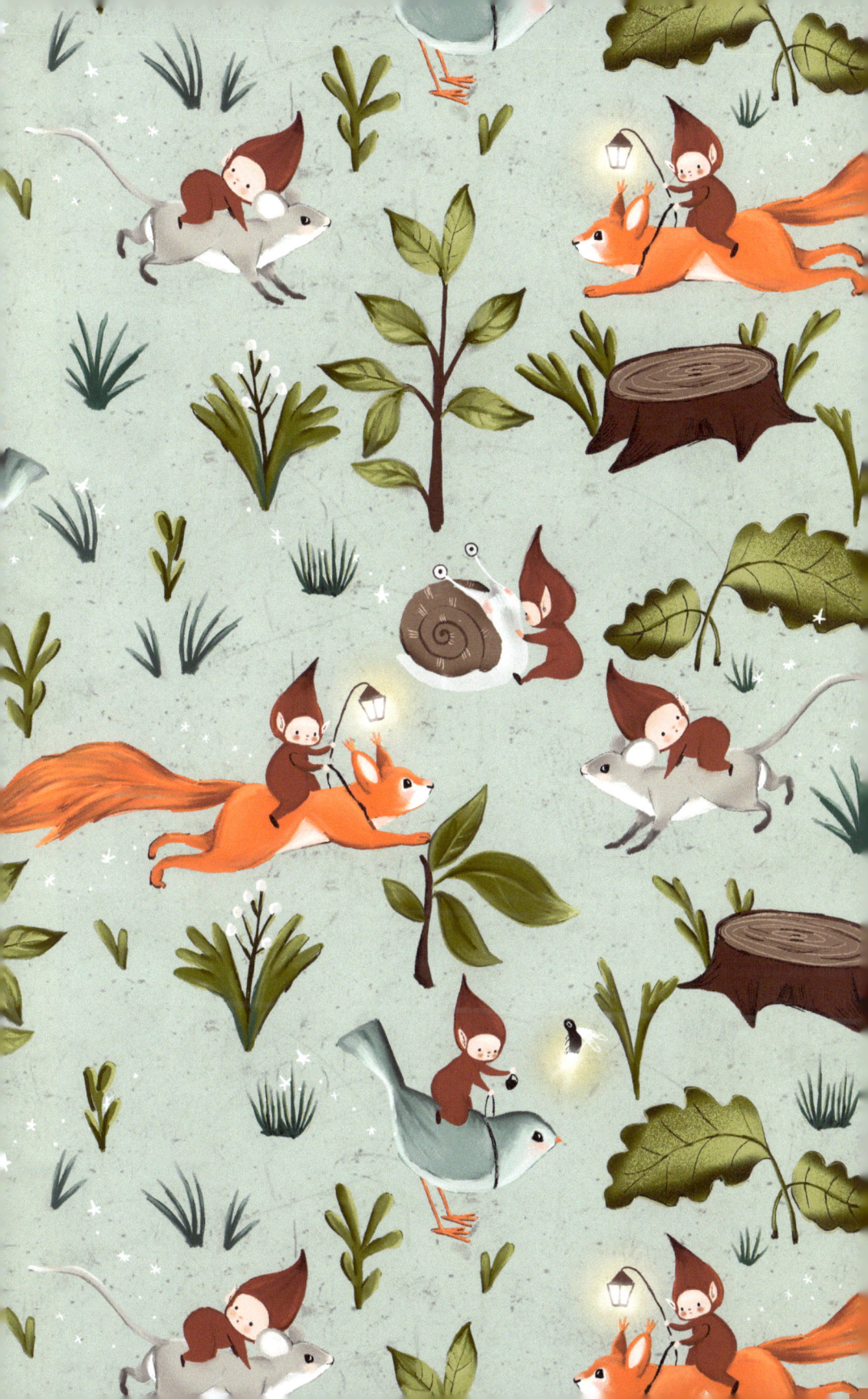

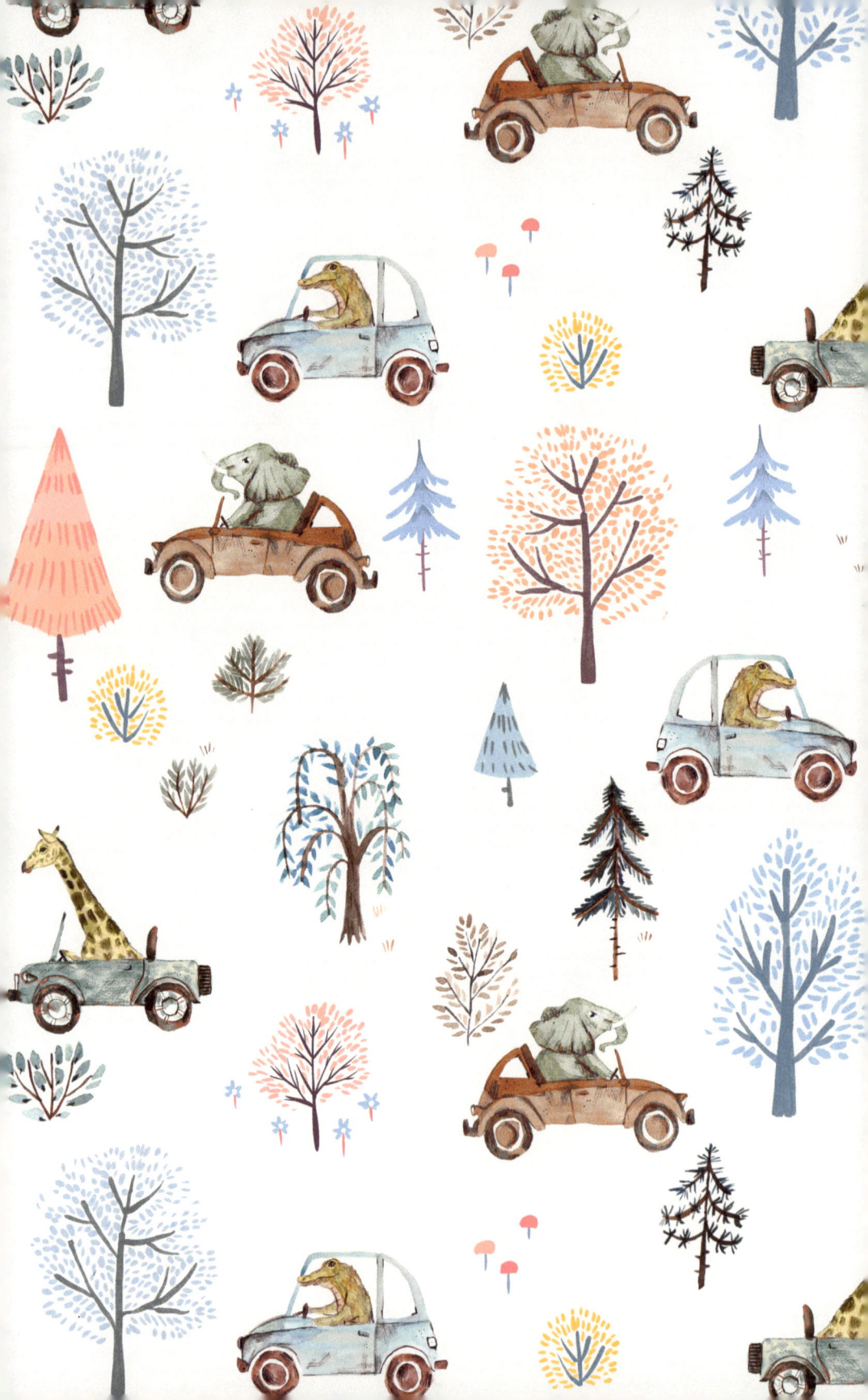

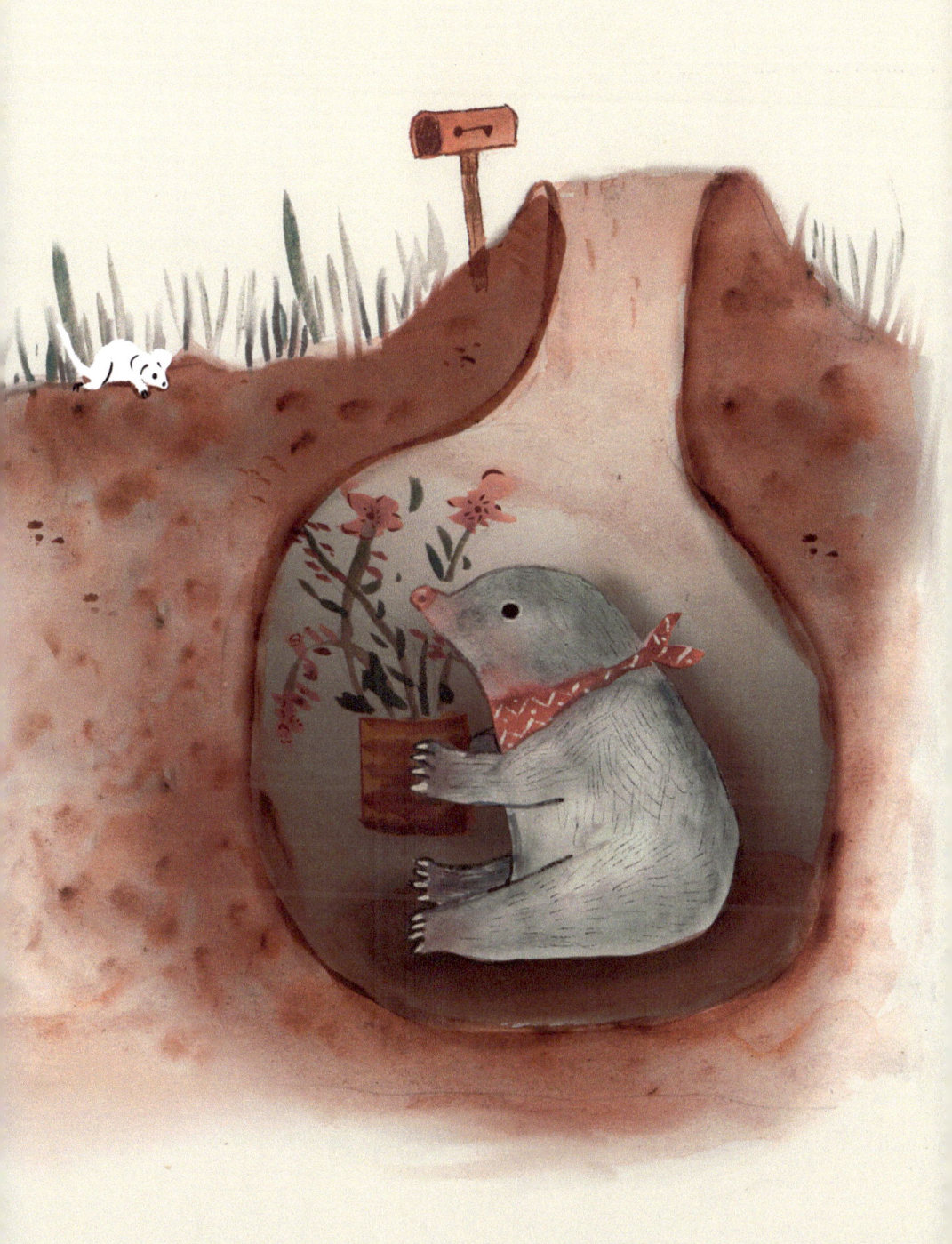

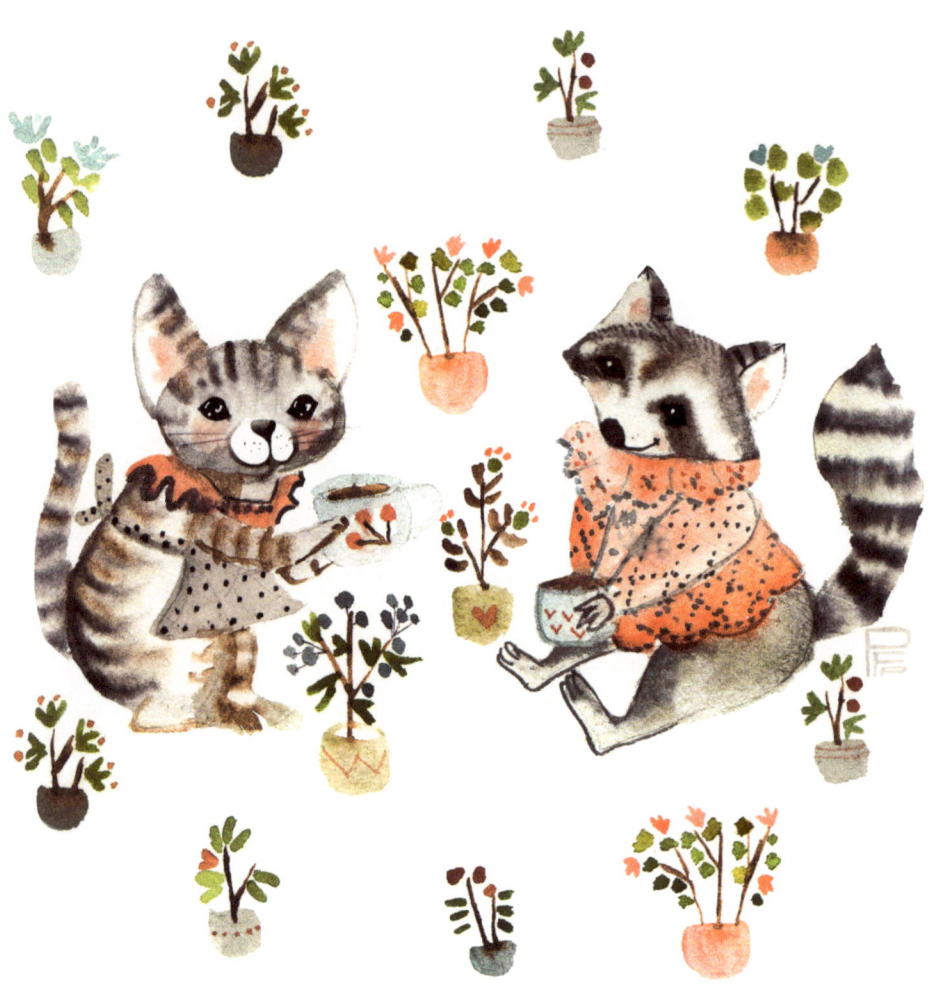

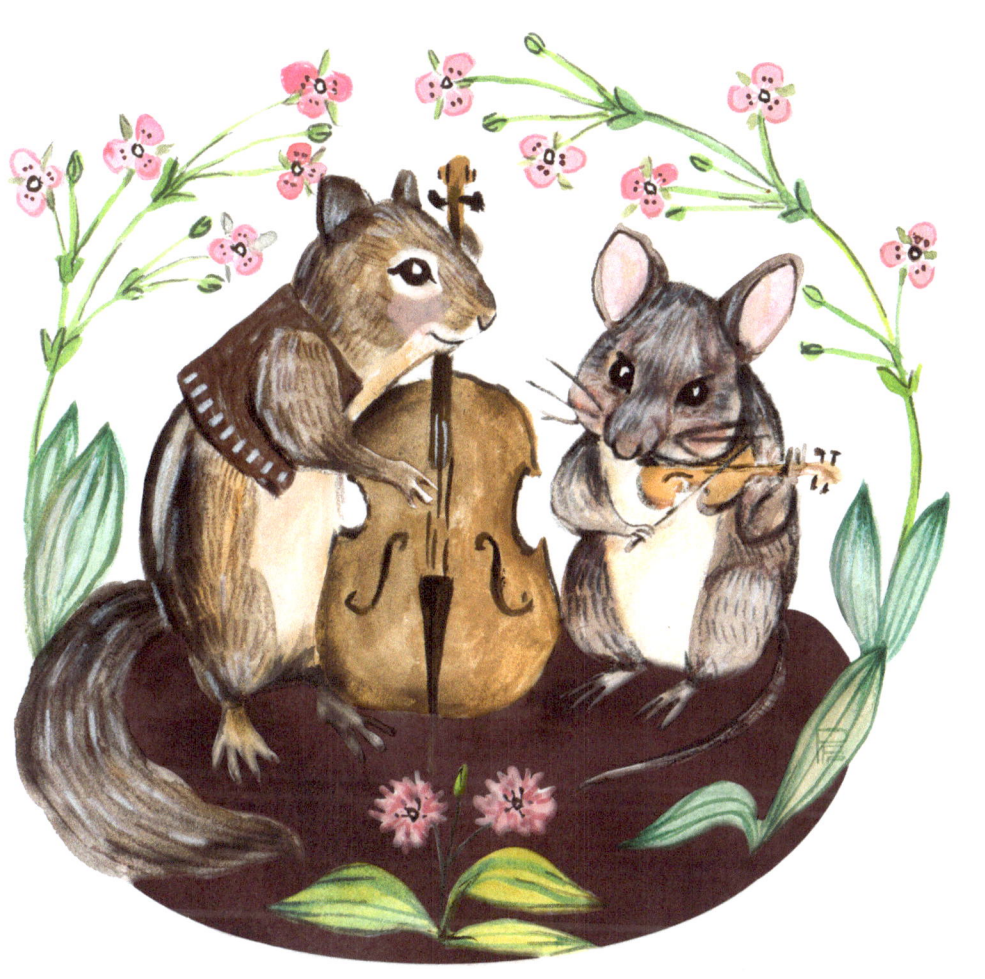

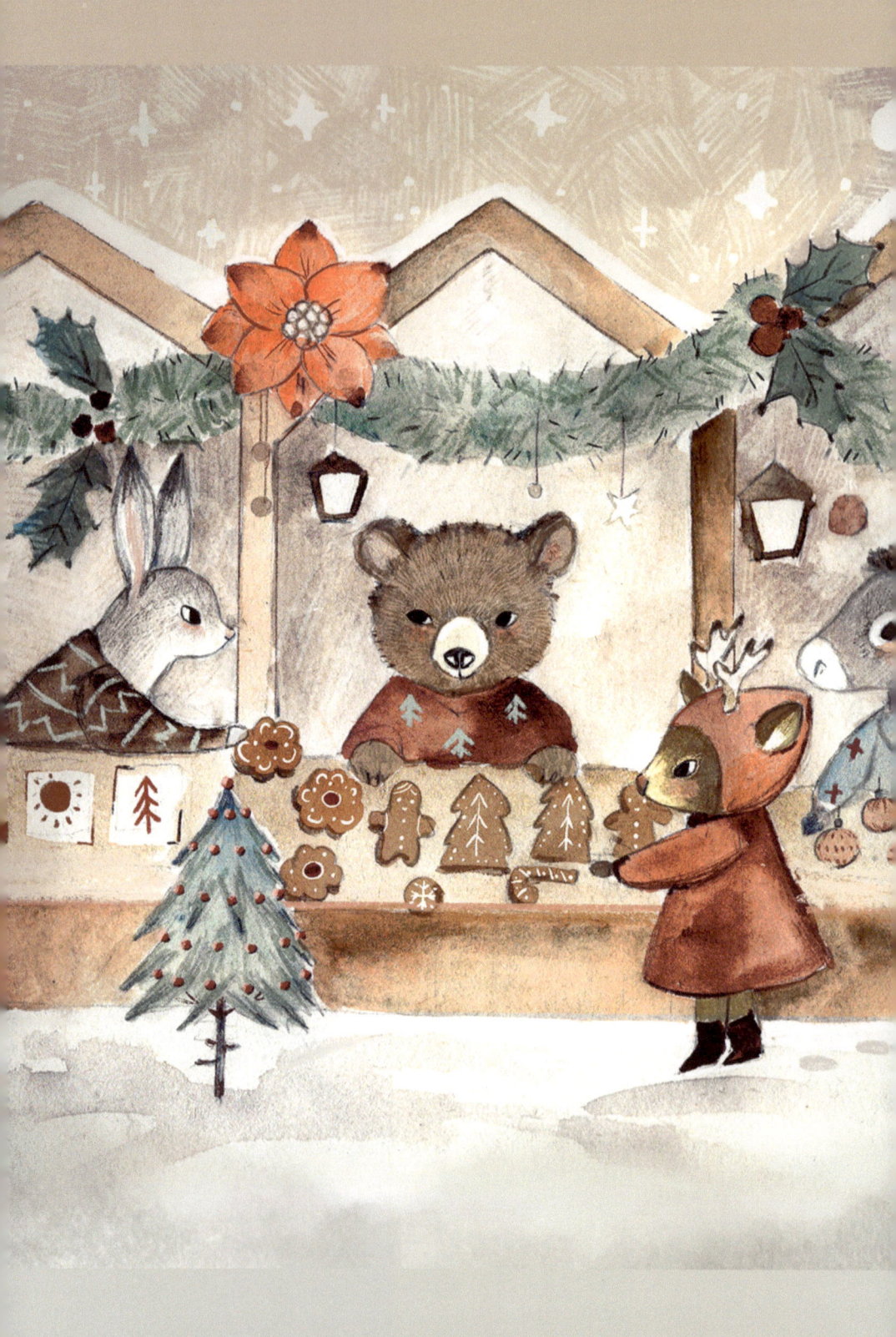

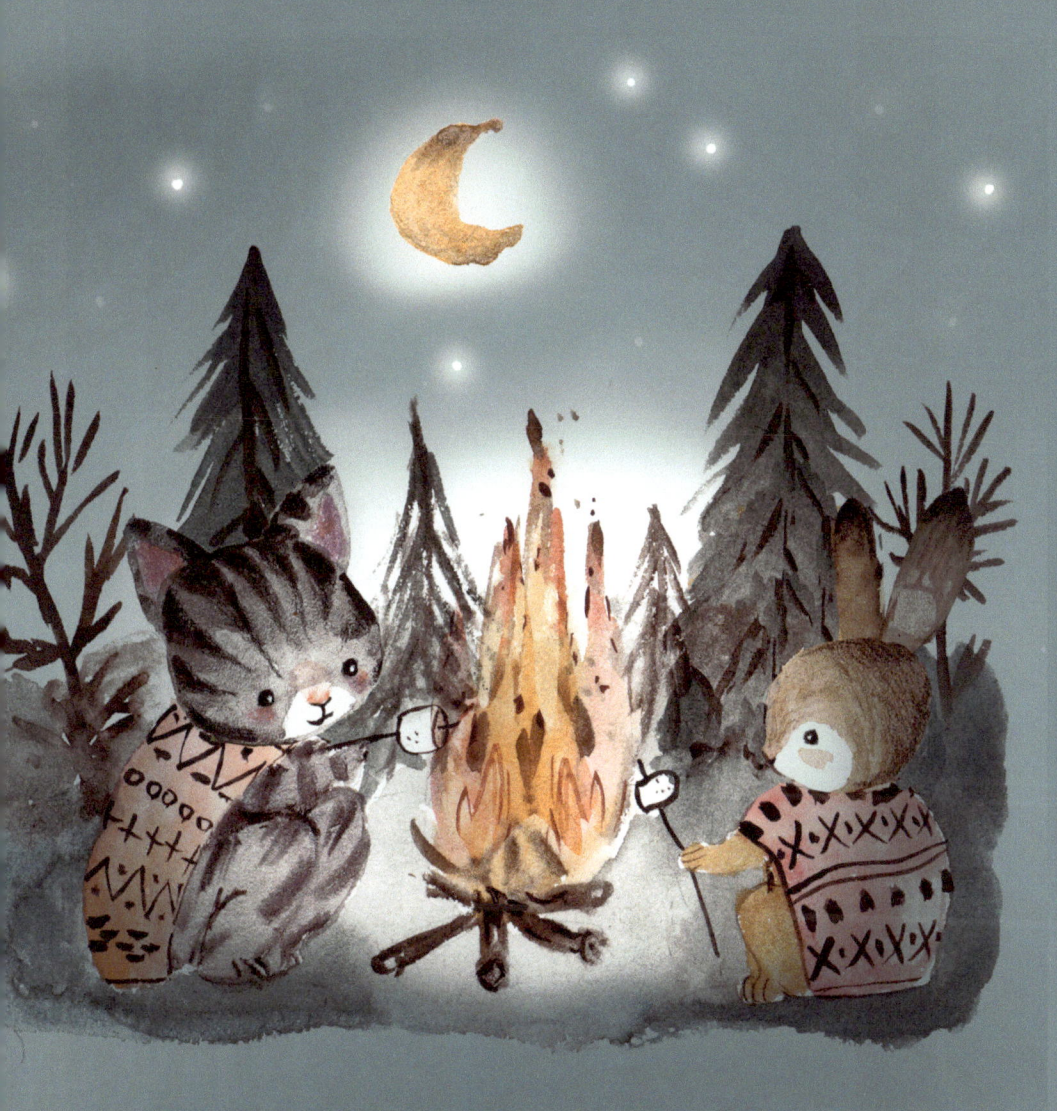

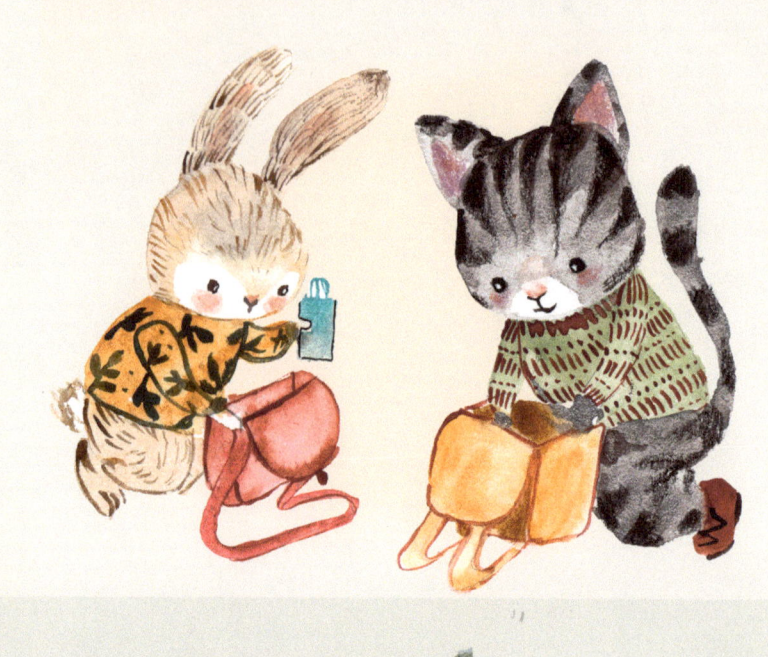

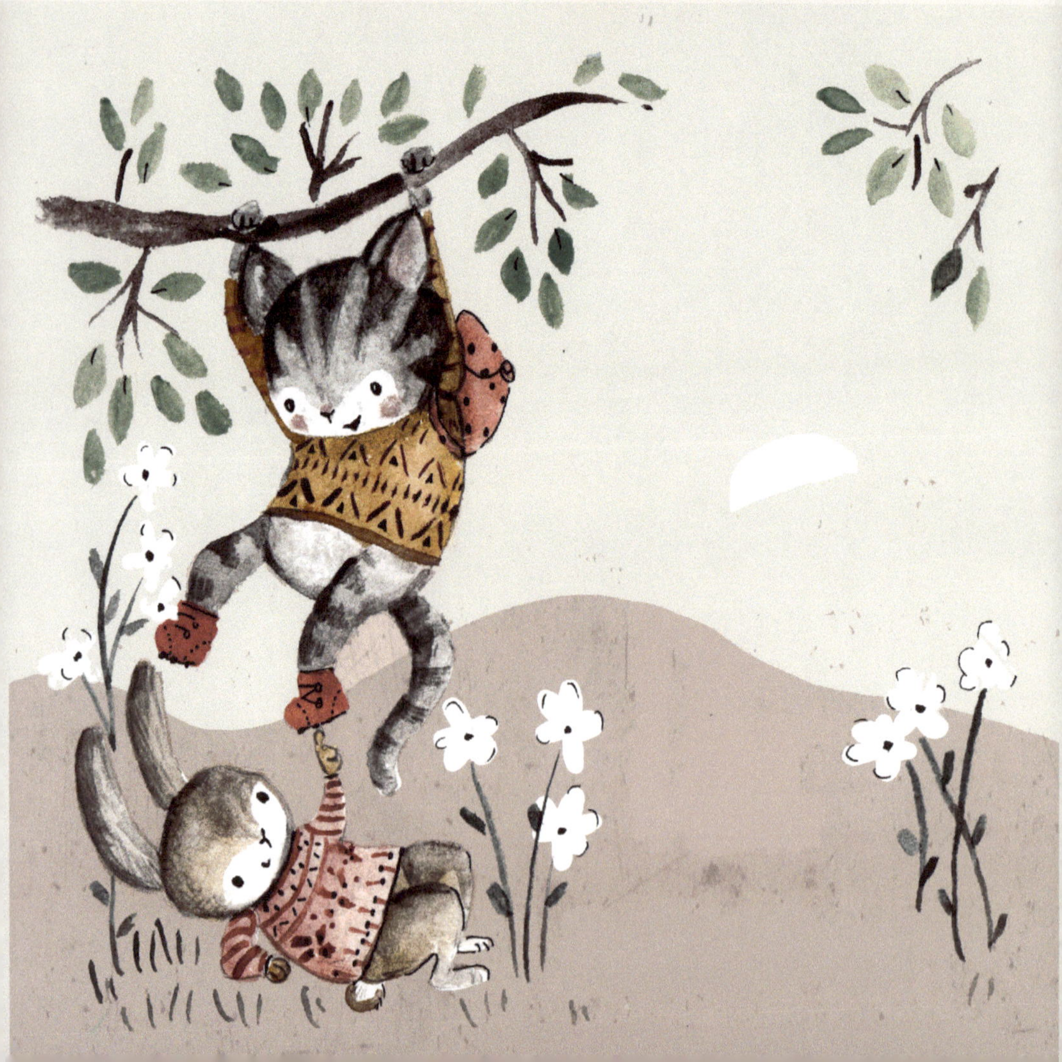

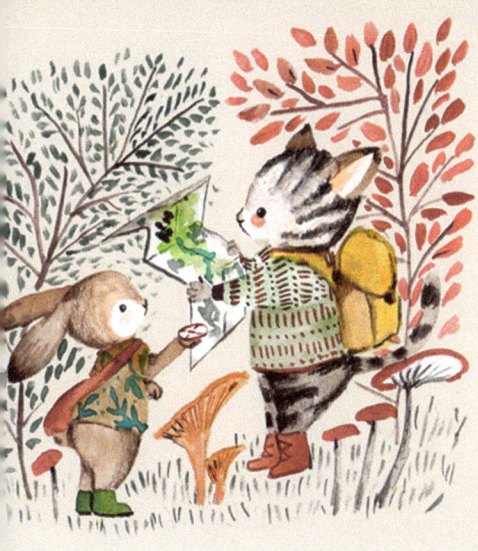
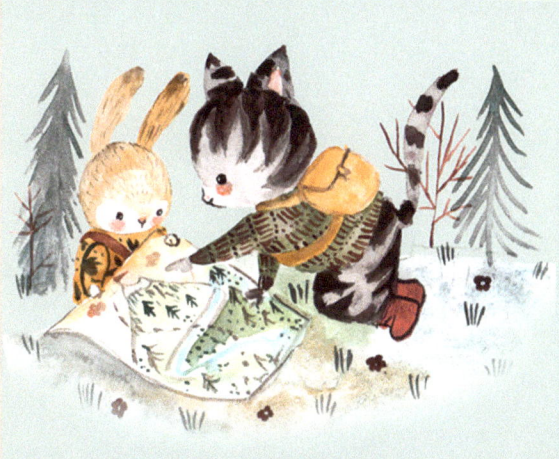
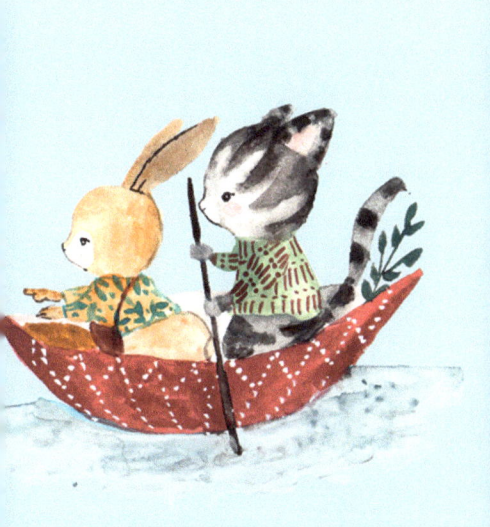
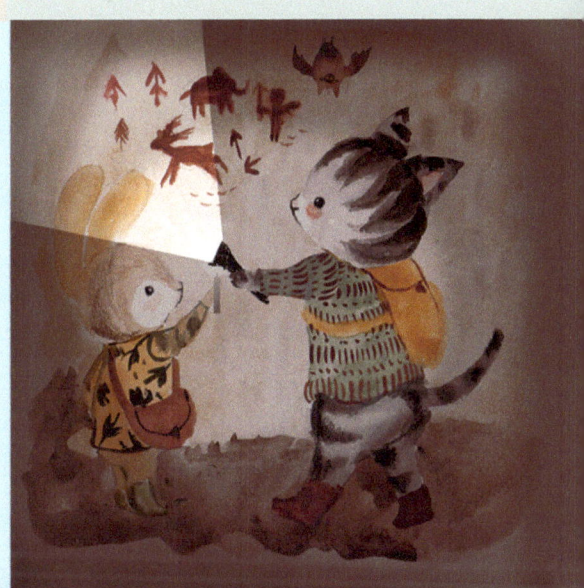
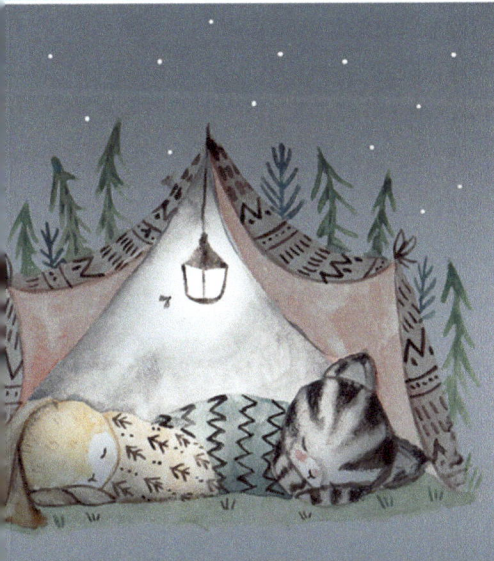
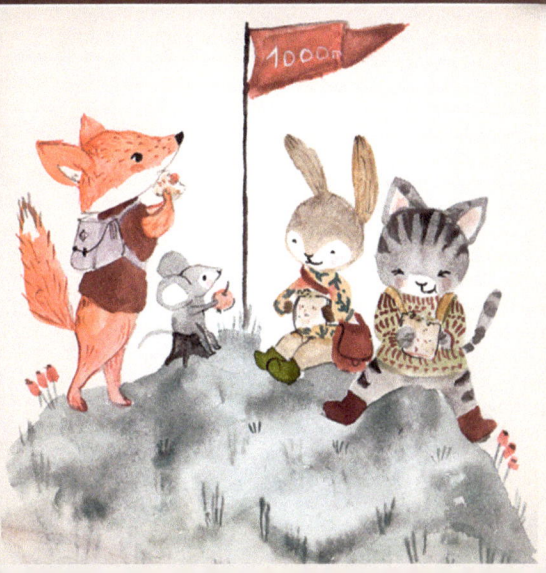

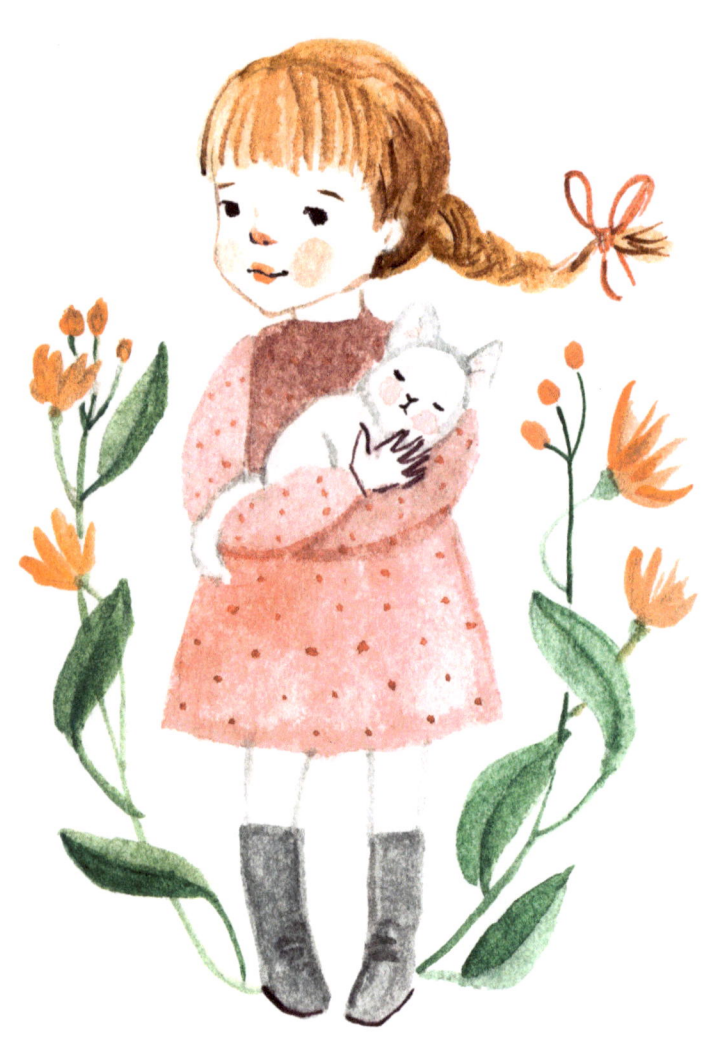

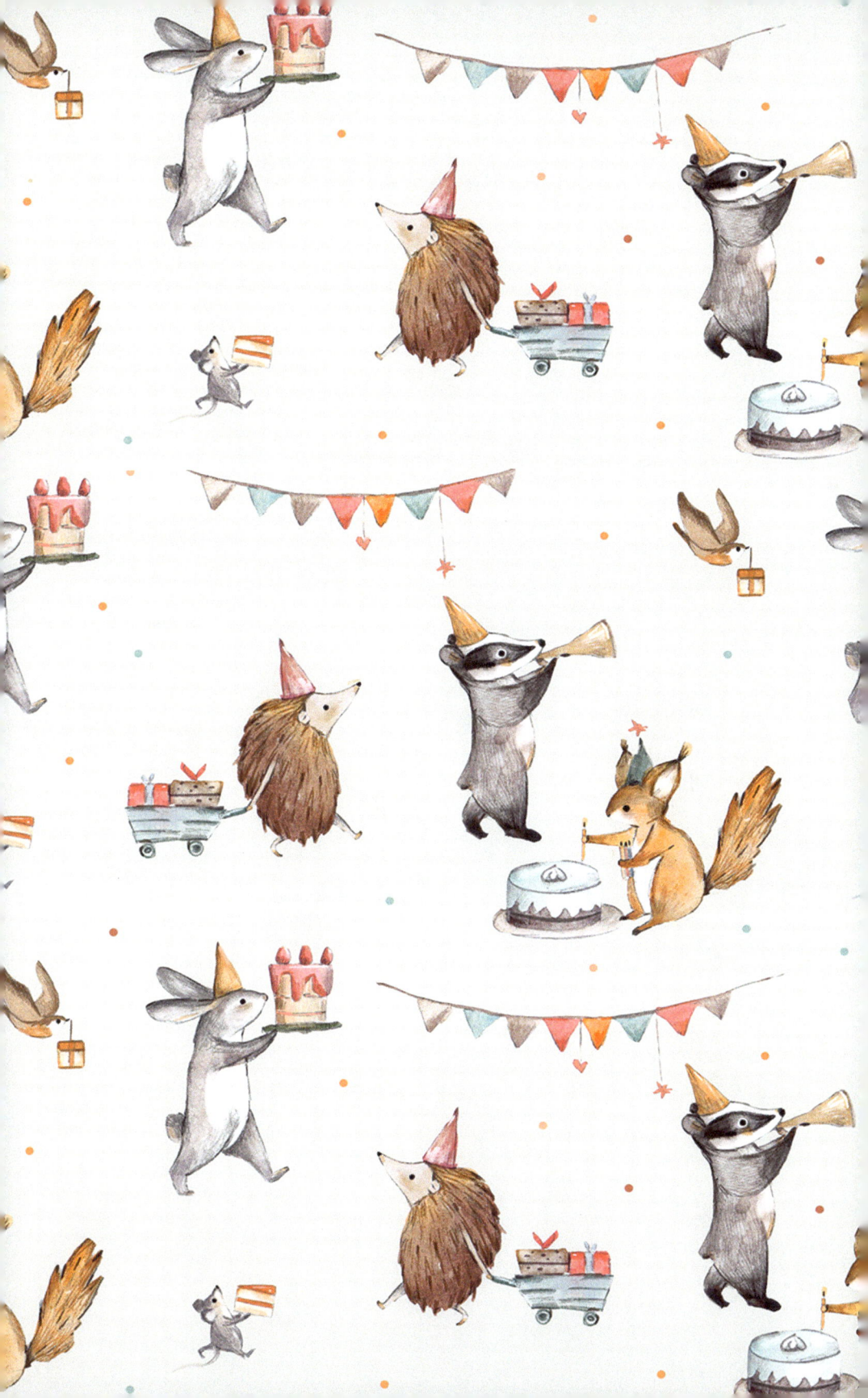

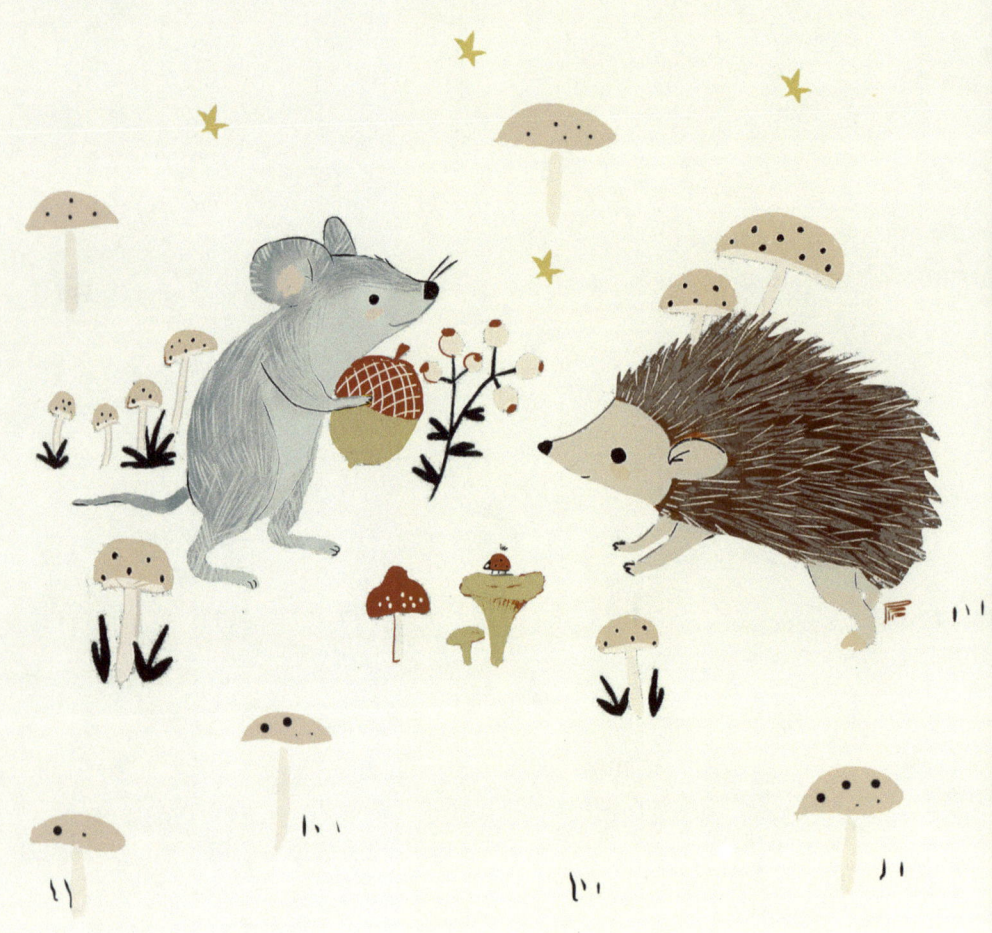

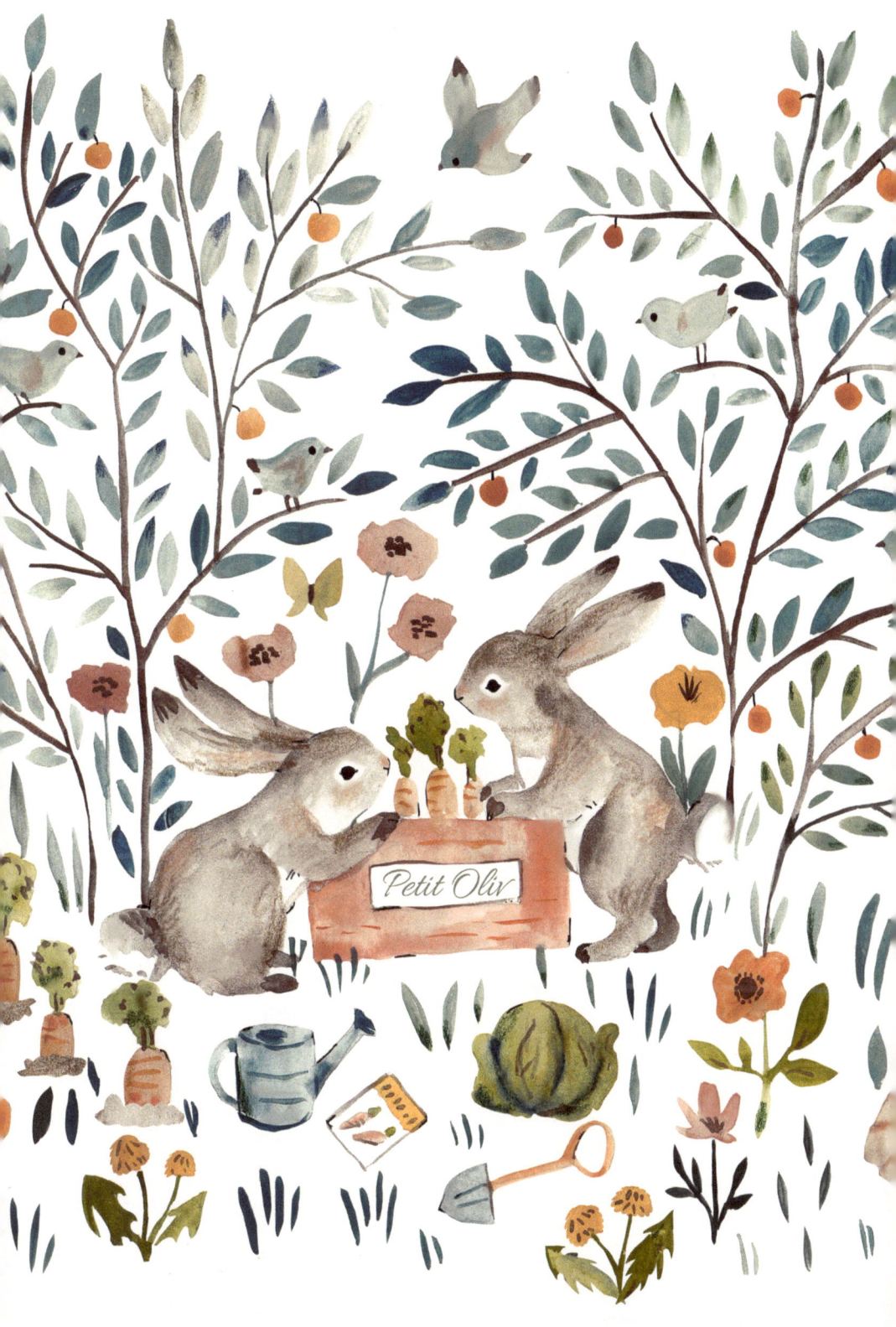

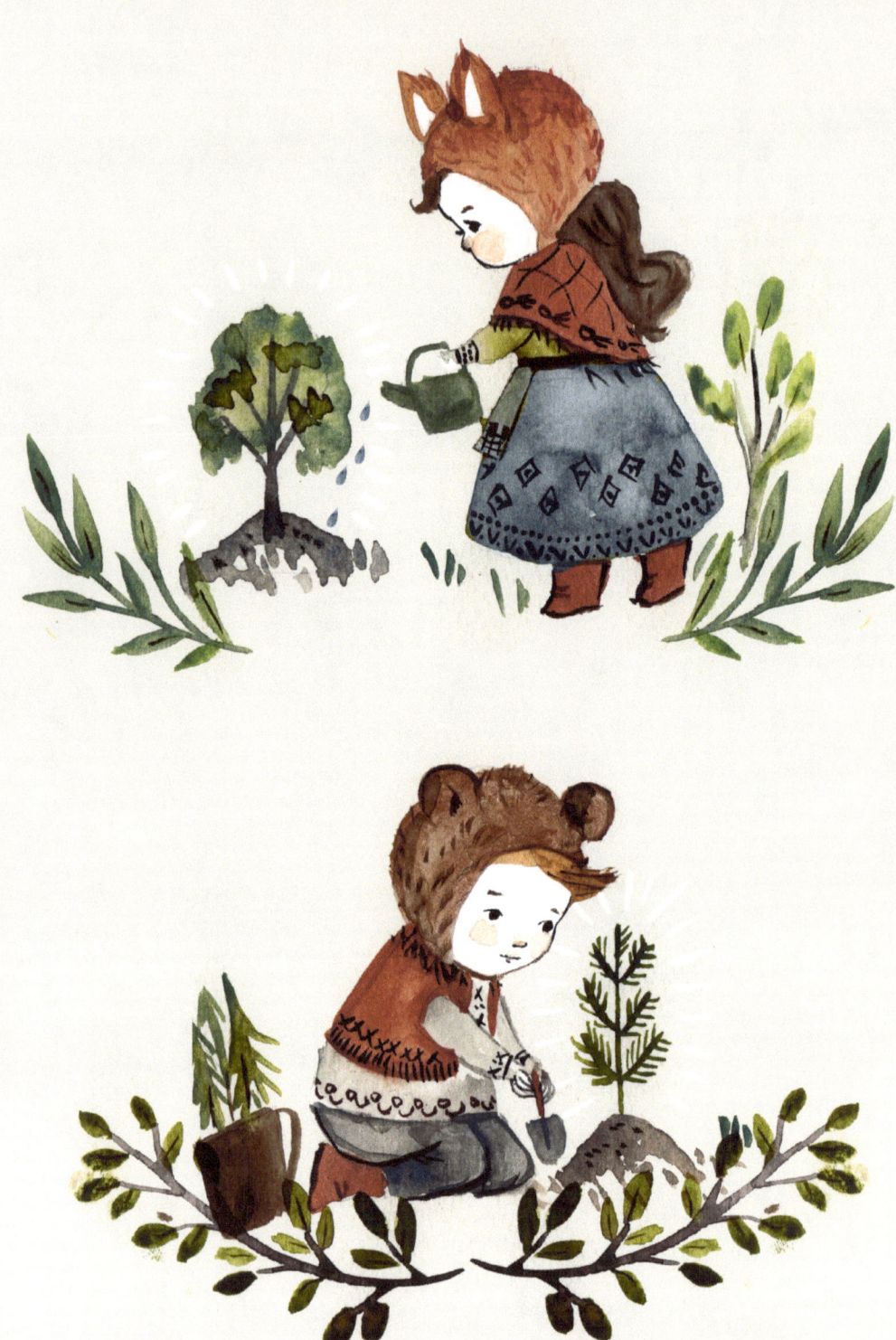

www.ingramcontent.com/pod-product-compliance
Lightning Source LLC
Chambersburg PA
CBHW040349220526
45473CB00009B/2829